KU-547-053

BRITAIN IN PICTURES
THE BRITISH PEOPLE IN PICTURES

THE LONDONER

GENERAL EDITOR
W. J. TURNER

AUTHOR'S NOTE

In devoting these few pages to the Londoner it has been possible to dwell only on such aspects of his character and history as have some relevance at the present time. The preponderance of the masculine pronoun is due solely to exigencies of space.

THE LONDONER

LADY NICHOLSON

*WITH
8 PLATES IN COLOUR
AND
20 ILLUSTRATIONS IN
BLACK & WHITE*

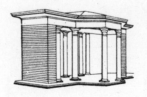

WILLIAM COLLINS OF LONDON
MCMXXXXIV

PRODUCED BY
ADPRINT LIMITED LONDON

PRINTED IN GREAT BRITAIN BY
WM. COLLINS SONS AND CO. LTD. GLASGOW
ON MELLOTEX BOOK PAPER MADE BY
TULLIS RUSSELL & CO. LTD. MARKINCH. SCOTLAND

LIST OF ILLUSTRATIONS

BLACK AND WHITE ILLUSTRATIONS

*Thanks for valuable help are due to the National Football Association and the
Greyhound Racing Association of Great Britain.*—AUTHOR

COVENT GARDEN : SHELLING PEAS
Water colour by Dorothy Belasco, 1938

I

LONDON is the largest city in the world, the largest port, the largest industrial town in England, and a great capital city. No other city on earth has so many facets, so many walks and ways of life. "London is a world by itself, . . . among the Londoners are so many nations differing in manners, customs, and religions, that the inhabitants themselves don't know a quarter of them," wrote Tom Brown in 1690 when the Londoners were not a million. Now, in the four million in the County of London, and four million more at least, in the vast receding nebulae of Greater London, the Londoner is hard to know and harder still to define ; not more than two-thirds of the present Londoners were born in London. Single trades by themselves are large enough to populate considerable towns ; the clerks are a third of all the clerks in England, and there are a quarter of a million shopkeepers, twelve thousand taximen (in normal times), ten thousand costermongers. There are Archbishops, bookies, policemen, newsmen, busmen, dustmen, all the professions (and some are very queer), business men, chairmen, directors, stockbrokers, typists, and heaven knows how many charladies, often mothers of their ten or thirteen, who wash all the floors and steps in London, dust all the desks, empty all the paper baskets each day before the chairmen can take the chair, the directors direct, the brokers broke or the typewriters click. And there are or were the idlers, whether members of the Drones' Club or the Hungerford, but total war has much diminished these.

In this immensity the Londoner, whoever he is, should be overwhelmed, but he is not, for the vastness of London is resolved into an infinity of smaller units, self-contained, that make life human and habitable. The twenty-eight boroughs, into which the County of London was divided in 1899, make the huge mass manageable, and gather up local feeling (and passion, too, sometimes) with what valuable effect Civil Defence and other war organisations have shown ; and there are many lesser organic groupings, innumerable old parishes and villages with their High Streets and taverns preserving a local centre, a sense of intimacy, and a strong individual character. No part of London is like any other. The City and Westminster are different continents, and beyond the City is a world which the West End seldom sees. In Chelsea people look like artists but may be something quite other. In Wapping, if you loiter you will be asked what ship you are waiting for, and you will cause surprise if you do not know when high tide is. In Clerkenwell people lean from upper windows to ask if they can help you to find the way. To people on one side of the river those on the other are aliens, suspect, "across the water." Local patriotism is strong ; people who had lost their homes in the blitz would refuse to leave the district. "Why should I let 'Itler get me out of Poplar ?" they would say, or it might be Bermondsey, or Stepney, or Lambeth, or Fulham, or Bethnal Green.

Begonia Brown : "The people of Camberwell are the pick of South London society ; the Peckham people are lower middle class, the scum of the earth."

Sir Orpheus : "Do not deceive yourself, my lord ; fire a shot at England, and Camberwell and Peckham will stand shoulder to shoulder."

The cockney, whoever he is, has first claim to be a Londoner, and even he is hard to capture. Traditionally he should be born within the sound of Bow Bells, a practice much in neglect of late, and most Londoners have grown up knowing their sound only by wireless. In past times cockney was a term of derision meaning someone pampered, petted, over-fed, as townees seem to rustics : "all born within the sound of Bow Bells are cockneys and buttered toasts,"

> "In cockneys' streets no mould is seen
> Pancakes are the shingles all . . .
> Running rivers great and small
> Of hypocras and ale and wine."

To the cartoonists of the last century, the cockney was a mean, pert, shabby person, inaspirate, with a vein of caustic repartee and no manners.

8

VIEW OF LONDON FROM THE THAMES, SHOWING THE TOWER

Oil painting by Samuel Scott, 1753

By courtesy of The Fine Art Society, London

BOROUGH HIGH STREET, SOUTHWARK
Water colour by William Knox, 1826

Latterly he has risen in esteem, thanks to the gracious art of Albert Chevalier, and, to many, he is the picturesque coster with his 'Arriet, the pearly with his queen, his painted cart, and his knowing moke or pony, ready to "knock 'em in the old Kent road," or chaffing, singing and hat-changing on the Heath on Bank Holiday or at Epsom on Derby Day. But the pearly is disappearing, and so too (like most native music) the cockney speech. People who were never born in London, or heard Bow Bells, now call themselves cockneys in sheer vainglory; so perhaps the word should shed all too particular, and also all derisive meanings, and return to its original meaning as a townee, but of the greatest town in the world, as short, or affectionate, for Londoner.

No city on earth has had more distinguished children, and they come most often, not from great houses but from unpretentious city homes and shops. Chaucer was born in the Vintry, Sir Thomas More in Milk Street, Herrick in Cheap, Donne (an ironmonger's son) and Milton, in Bread Street; Stow, the City's great antiquary, who boasted that he never wrote anything in "malice, fear or favour," was the son of a Cornhill tailor. Defoe came from a butcher's shop in Cripplegate, Alexander Pope from a linendraper's, Faraday served in a stationer's shop. From just such homes all over modern London come the heroes of the present war.

There are, too, great Londoners who never lived at all, but are none the less immortal : Falstaff, John Gilpin, Pickwick and their kind. There have been great clowns, from Tarlton to Dan Leno and Chaplin, authentic Londoners ; and sometimes quite solid reality has ascended to the fabulous, as in the case of Whittington and his Cat.

And above all stand three who excelled in the art of being a Londoner (only one was born in London) Samuel Pepys, Samuel Johnson, and Charles Lamb.

If a typical London character is hard to find, certain qualities stand out, despite the general diversity. As a citizen of no mean city the Londoner, has, in modern times, urbanity, style, a certain sophistication and a high standard. He is a fine craftsman, especially in the old London trades, leather-work, saddlery, furs, the best jewellery, musical and surgical instruments; and, till recently, the best Sheffield cutlery came to London to be finished. He has, opportunely, great patience and philosophy ; a person in a hurry, or who shows impatience in a queue, or anywhere at all in London gets little sympathy and no help. He is kind to foreigners and proud of the passing strangers now so numerous in his midst. In former times he was less hospitable, when he had to wrest his trade from the foreign merchants established in his city. At any time enemy (or late enemy) aliens might be mobbed in the streets as Voltaire was, till he made a neat speech apologising for not having been born a Londoner. As for the foreigners, since the French refugees from the Revocation of the Edict

9

STREET FIGHT
Coloured aquatint by G. and R. Cruikshank, 1821

of Nantes brought their silk-weaving to Spitalfields, they have often preferred life in London to the persecutions so frequent upon the continent; and the French and Italians in Soho, the Jews of Whitechapel and Stepney are as good Londoners as any, and their exotic atmosphere adds a bright touch of colour to the London scene.

Charity is a London tradition, nowhere else is so much money given for disasters over the whole world. There is a softness of heart, too, for those lesser Londoners, the sparrows, the pigeons, the seagulls, the swans, the ducks in the parks, for whom there is cake and bread even in time of dearth. And among the Londoner's most amiable fancies is to contrive a scrap of country life in odd unexpected corners. Prize gardens and prize dahlias spring in most unlikely places, broad beans and tomatoes flourish upon the rubbish of the blitz. Modern, convenient flats make poor headway against the profound passion for rabbits, pigeons, chickens, and other backyard fauna, and blitzed ruins bring forth pigs.

As for amusements and sports, no people have had so many; through all ages they have been a large part of the Londoner's life, accompanied, it must be confessed, with a great deal of gambling, and betting on cock-fighting, wrestling, boxing, racing of all kinds, and even on bowls, and now in football pools and on his dearest, youngest sport, dog-racing. But if the propensity for betting is to be deplored, there is evidence that its recent undeniable increase, with football pools and dogs, is steadily superseding the Londoner's old propensity for drink.

For a drunkard, alas, the Londoner has been in the past. Drinking and fires were the only plagues of London, according to William Fitzstephen, who has left us a description of London in the twelfth century. In the sixteenth century, according to a German, the Londoners in their cups would rush up the steeples and ring the bells. There have always been too many taverns; in 1589 there were a thousand in the City of London and Lord Chancellor Bacon suggested to the Lord Mayor that he might close a few, and successive Mayors tried to check and limit the drinking, but in vain. In Dickens's time there was a tavern to every sixty houses, and gin shops with thousands of callers a day. But if the Thames is liquid history, so surely are London's taverns. The *Tabard*, the *Boar's Head* in Eastcheap, the *Mermaid* with its patrons Shakespeare, Beaumont, Ben Jonson, Raleigh, Donne ("what things have we seen done at the Mermaid"), the *Devil* in Fleet Street where Ben Jonson held court in the great Apollo Room which saw Pepys, Hogarth, Dr. Johnson and Sir Joshua Reynolds; the *Mitres*, the *Turk's Head*, and all the *Suns*, *Crowns*, *Swans*, with their clientele of poets, playwrights and essayists, as well as good plain folk; they are a big part of London's history. "Would that I were in a London ale-house and safe" cries the Boy at Harfleur. As for brewers, what would Dr. Johnson have done without the Thrales?

The Londoners have always been regarded, especially by foreigners, as fighters. In 993 they defeated the Danes "with more slaughter and harm than they thought townsmen could inflict." "The English," says Froissart, "are the worst people in the world, the most obstinate and presumptuous, and of all England the Londoners are the worst . . . for they are bold and courageous, and the more their blood is spilled the greater is their courage." Street fighting was much practised through the seventeenth and eighteenth centuries; not rough uncivil battling but with rules, the crowd forming a ring to see fair play. "Tout ce qui s'appelle Combat, est une chose délicieuse aux Anglais," was a French comment on the London streets, and in 1812 a Russian, at a time when Russians were "much caressed here," was amazed at the democratic manner of the fighting, for a gentleman could fight a butcher boy and no one must interfere even if the gentleman got the worst. "The genius of the people tends that way."

II

ALFRED the Great may be said to have made London, when, in 886 he recovered it from the Danes, rebuilt the walls, brought in population from the Home Counties, and generally persuaded the Londoners that it was their duty to keep the Danes out of south eastern England, or at any rate out of their town. Hitherto, since the departure of the Romans, they had made no attempt to defend themselves; at each Saxon raid they just melted away, returning when the danger was over, and the fine town which in Roman times had swarmed, Tacitus said, with merchants and travellers, had become a poor decayed place with its walls in ruins. When the Danes came they easily occupied it, but when Alfred had taken the situation in hand it held off the Danes for a century, and fell only by treachery and when the rest of England had capitulated.

The Londoners learned Alfred's lesson well. Inside the neat circuit of their walls, which time has not effaced, they developed a most exemplary aptitude for their own defence, and that of their trade, their liberties and privileges. If, at times, their independence has looked almost like isolationism, it must be remembered that the government of England, since the time of Edward the Confessor, has been at Westminster, never in the City of London. The main objects of the Londoners have always been their trade, their liberties, and the proper conduct within the City of a pleasant life of industry, sport, pageantry, and the free practice of their religion, with peace and orderly rule to secure them. To these blameless objectives a principal difficulty has often been their own kings, in early times rapacious, war-mongering, regarding the City as a place unblushingly to plunder. The Londoners accepted the sovereigns as a divine, if sometimes awkward, institution, but estimated each sovereign ruthlessly by the amount of money he demanded, what it was for, when, whether and how he paid or made return. They would refuse money on occasion without a qualm, and go to the Tower rather than pay. Over the privileges of sole judicial authority and the sole right to arrest and punish offenders within the gates, they carried on a running fight with the Crown, even with Parliament, down to the eighteenth century, with frequent riot and bloodshed.

Foreigners, beside kings, were a difficulty. From the tenth century, Germans of the Hansa League had a settlement, the "Steelyard" in the City close to the Bridge, and the French Vintners had a wharf at the Wall Brook, before the Conquest. Later the finance of London was in the hands of the Jews (till their expulsion under Edward I), and then of the Lombards, till Edward III, despoiling them, gave the great London merchants a chance to do their own banking. Flemish weavers found their way in, to the dismay of the craftsmen, and anti-foreign riots were a commonplace.

So, between kings and foreigners the Londoners picked their way through the middle ages, wading through all the reigns of the Williams,

THE BATTLE OF HASTINGS
Detail from the Bayeux Tapestry, Eleventh Century

the Henrys, the Edwards, the Richards, with loyal optimism (usually soon to be disappointed), and lavish pageantry at each accession, never losing sight of their purpose, gaining a charter here, a privilege there, building up, not an ordinary mediaeval city, but the pattern and foundation of the London we know to-day, with the glamour of its traditions and immense power of resistance.

Even before the Conquest, they had acquired wealth and prestige, and some experience of king-making. They fought at Hastings, but when disaster befell they accepted William with philosophy and William accepted them with a most comprehensive, and positively deferential charter, often described as a Treaty, upon which all the rights of the City of London rest.

"William the King greets William the Bishop, and Gosfregh the Port-Reeve and all the Burghers within London, both French and English, friend-like ; and I give you to know, that ye be of all those Laws worthy that ye were in King Edward's day. And I will suffer no man to do you any wrong. God keep you."

He also built the White Tower in order to keep an eye on the independent Londoners.

From Henry I London got the right to choose its Sheriffs and from King John recognition of the "Commune" of London (the first that is heard of it) and, for the first time, the right of the Court of Aldermen to choose a Mayor, "a person faithful and discreet fit for government of the City" ; and in Magna Carta a clause was inserted confirming all the

13

City's "ancient liberties and customs both by land and water." Henceforward London is almost a city-state, which neither the sovereign nor his armed forces may enter without permission, in which the Lord Mayor ("Lord" was added later) takes precedence of everyone except the sovereign. "Come what may," shouted an excited citizen, "Londoners shall have no king but their Mayor."

With Richard I (in whom the Londoners found no glamour) and Henry III there was ceaseless friction over money, and mutual dislike. For Simon de Montfort, with his ideas of parliamentary government, the Londoners rose against Henry and fought heroically at Lewes. They had a principal part in deposing Richard II : when he heard that the Londoners had come to Flint castle to take him, he capitulated in terror, a sad ending to a reign begun as the "Londoners' king" when he faced Wat Tyler's rebels gallantly in Smithfield. Henry V, expensive as he was, held the Londoners' affections from first to last and at every event of his reign was accorded their most lavish pageantry. They so hated the dismal meaningless Wars of the Roses that they accepted Edward IV thankfully. He loved London, including the London ladies, notably the beautiful Jane Shore, amusing, lively, friendly, a perfect queen of cockneys. They even acclaimed Richard III, in face of an alternative monarch aged thirteen. And if their preferences in kings seem occasionally strange, an explanation is usually to be found in the possible alternative, or some recent disastrous experience.

The fourteenth century, despite the Hundred Years' War, was a good time for London : the Livery Companies got their charters. There had not, of course, been perfect unity and peace, for the city offices were in the hands of the semi-aristocratic merchant class, while the craftsmen and journeymen were without a voice in the city government, or protection for their trades. They had broken out in a riot in 1190, led by William of the Long Beard, "saviour of the people ;" they opened the gates to Simon de Montfort, and in 1262 forced their way into the town mote, threw out the Aldermen, and elected a Mayor of their own. There were riots, too, against foreigners and Jews. Trade associations existed, but unrecognised and repressed, as subversive and dangerous. Owing to the Black Death, however, which created a severe labour shortage, they gained strength, and in Edward III's reign four great guilds got their charters : Goldsmiths', Merchant Taylors', Skinners', and Fishmongers'. By 1362 there were thirty-two such guilds ; seventy-six are in existence to-day. Each had its livery, and complete control of its "mistery" (mastery) both the manufacture and the sale of its product. The charters provide for the quality of the material and the work and conditions of sale. Bad articles, blankets or hats, were to be burned, and goods must not be sold by candlelight. There were rules for apprenticeship; the Warden inspected and supervised, and workmen were forbidden to make "covins or conspiracies"

14

TITLEPAGE OF THE CHARTER BOOK OF THE BARBER-SURGEONS, 1605
Facsimile from Sidney Young's *Annals of the Barber Surgeons
of London*, 1890

to raise prices. The movement has been hailed as democratic; in fact, by the inclusion of merchant as well as craftsmen—a custom peculiar to London—the merchants, who had most of the wealth, inevitably got control of the Companies, while the journeymen remained outside, without rights of any kind. But there were compensations: the crafts acquired great power and great wealth, the franchise of the City was obtained only by enrolment in the craft, and the enrolled craftsman was a freeman of the City. To-day it is still the Liverymen of the Companies who choose the Sheriffs and the Lord Mayor. Even in their attentuated modern form they are not merely part of the City's heritage, like its charities and traditional ceremonial, but essential to the civic structure.

15

Our first clear picture of London is Fitzstephen's in 1180. There are thirteen great religious foundations, and a hundred and thirty-six parish churches. St. Paul's is being rebuilt, the "greatest church in Europe," a hundred feet longer than Wren's great church, and London Bridge is being rebuilt in stone, to last, barring a few misadventures with tide and flood, till the nineteenth century. St. Bartholomew's, built by Rahere, Henry I's repentant jester, is sixty years old, the Knights of St. John are in Clerkenwell, the Templars at the "Temple" on the river bank. There are gardens of the citizens in the suburbs, with fruit trees and water-mills that clack pleasantly, and on summer evenings people stroll out to the springs in the meadows at Clerkenwell, Holywell and St. Clement's. Every day the craftsmen and vendors of goods are in their appointed quarters. There is an immense variety of sports ; bear and bull-baiting, cock-fighting (for school boys) water quintain on the river at which everyone in the boats and on the Bridge roars with laughter when the players fall in the water. When Moorfields are frozen there is skating and a very rough game of single-stick ; in Smithfield horse-shows and races. Football is a favourite game ; each school and craft has its team, and the older men ride out to watch the games and cheer. Near the river is a cook-shop "among the wine-shops," open day and night, with roast, fried and boiled, ready to provide for anybody, and to supply citizens who may have unexpected guests at home. The matrons are most respectable, Fitzstephen assures us, and there are three great schools (St. Paul's, Westminster and St. Saviour's, Southwark) where the boys hold inter-collegiate debates on grammar. There is much festivity, hospitality and charity, in fact, "the only inconveniences are the immoderate drinking and fires."

Except for the drinking, Fitzstephen omits the seamy side of life ; there must surely have been gambling and betting on the cocks, the horses and the games. There were, too, thieves and pick-pockets, filthy prisons and compters (lock-ups), the unrest of the unenfranchised journeymen, the stews, mostly in Bankside, kept by "Froes of Flanders, since English people disdain to be bawds," which Henry II had regulated only a few years before. But the picture, as far as it goes, is of vitality, prosperity and strong corporate life.

The glamour of London in the later middle ages brought the younger sons of country families to seek their fortunes. There were great mayors, and great citizens, living in houses (Crosby Hall is the dining hall of one of them) which would be reckoned as palaces in any age. Sir Henry Picard, in his great house in the Vintry, entertained Edward III, the King of Scots, the King of Cyprus and the Prince of Wales, while Lady Picard kept open house upstairs. At the dicing after dinner, when the King of Cyprus (a bad loser) would not pay his debts, Picard returned him what he had lost. In 1378 John Philpot, Mayor, put to sea with a fleet to deal with Scottish pirates in the North Sea, and defeated them off

RICHARD WHITTINGTON, d. 1423
Engraving by R. Elstbrack, c. 1571—after 1625

Scarborough, taking all their ships and prizes, and some Spanish ships which had joined them. Sir Richard Walworth, who sat his horse in Smithfield against Wat Tyler's rebels with the king, and struck down Tyler with his own hand (he also owned stews in Bankside), is a fierce but distinguished figure. Sir Richard Whittington, four times Lord Mayor (not three), is even more romantic in reality than in pantomime. He was banker to Henry IV and Henry V; the latter with Queen Isabella he entertained at his house in the City, with gold plate on the tables,

17

scented wood on the fire, before which the Cat or one of its descendants was no doubt sleeping, and after dinner he threw upon the fire bills for £60,000 which the king owed him. He instituted proceedings against the Brewers' Company for selling "dear ale," and won the case with costs.

Like many others he spent and left enormous sums in benefactions for public conduits, libraries, institutions. His executors founded the college of St. Spirit and St. Mary on College Hill, rebuilt St. Bartholomew's, glazed and paved the Guildhall (begun in 1411 by Thomas Knowles, a Grocer), and improved the prisons.

In the fourteenth century Chaucer was living over Aldgate, and the extraordinarily high level of culture is seen in the talk of the host and the Pilgrims in the *Canterbury Tales*. Schools multiplied, John Carpenter, Whittington's executor, founded the City School, now the City of London School; Henry VI founded eight grammar schools. Until the Dissolution, the schools used to hold a debate on grammar under a tree in Smithfield, in which the boys of St. Antony's usually won. Afterwards they fought in the streets with satchels of books "many times in heaps," and the Antonines called the Paulines pigeons because of the pigeons at St. Paul's, and the Paulines called the Antonines pigs, because St. Antony had a pig. When Caxton, who had been the Mercers' Flanders agent, brought his printing press to Westminster, he could scarcely meet the demand for his books.

For the 100,000 (or thereabouts) citizens packed within the walls, life was neighbourly and intimate, and the common punishments, the stocks and the pillory, show the torment of having to stand the neighbours' ridicule. Rich and poor lived close together, not in separate districts. Relief of poverty and infirmity was everybody's business; the wealthy citizen had to provide everything now provided by authority, from hospitals to supplies in time of dearth. Even the poor journeymen loved their town and, in Wat Tyler's rebellion and that of Jack Cade, having opened the gates to the rebels, turned against them when they saw their city being looted. Inclined to Lollardry, they sacked John of Gaunt's Palace of the Savoy when he took Wycliffe's part against their own bishop. In most of their upheavals the apprentices joined them; in their excitability and independence they were like the student class of continental towns; factious and turbulent, they would seize their clubs and rush to join in any fray. They were also idle, foppish, thieving, fond of dancing, music and ladies; or so Chaucer said.

The main centre of life was Cheap (Cheapside) the only broad thoroughfare, and the general market. Life in the narrow streets was noisy and lively with musicians, tumblers, jugglers, preaching friars, pigs, ordinary people, cooks and shopkeepers crying their wares, "ripe strawberries," "hot sheep's feet," "roast ribs of beef," and good wine was a penny a pint. All that was known of sanitation was piles of filth lying about. The good

A MARRIAGE FETE AT BERMONDSEY
Oil Painting by Joris Hoefnagel, 1545-1600

things impressed strangers, who, "for lack of money could never speed."
Even the surnames have a convivial sound : Buck and Piggesflesh, Golly-
Lolly, Spillwine, Brokedisher. The ladies were more refined with Swan-
hilda, Diamanda, Cassandra, Theophania.

Sports continued as in Fitzstephen's time ; football was forbidden to
Liverymen as undignified, while the "better sort" played tennis. A wrestling
match at St. Giles in the Fields ended on one occasion in an unfortunate
"hurly-burly" with the Westminster team. The fairs, St. Bartholomew's,
May Fair, Southwark, were in full swing. At Christmas the whole town
was decked with holly, ivy and bays ; on May Day everyone went out
early to get flowers and boughs, there were maypoles in every parish
and the great shaft was set up at St. Andrew's "Undershaft." On St.
John's Eve every house hung out lamps, and doors were "shadowed with
green birch, fennel, orpin and white lilies," with garlands of other flowers,
and there were bonfires and tables set in the streets by the "wealthier sort"
with sweet bread and meat and wine for the neighbours, and for chance
comers, too. The pageantry and the "ridings" on great days were among
the most cherished pleasures, when every class of the community had its

special dress, ordained for the occasion, scarlet or white or both with the craft symbols on the craftsmen's sleeves ; and even the journeymen had something. The Aldermen were magnificent in their velvet and say and sandal sometimes spangled with stars, and with gold chains, and the Lord Mayor in black velvet with a great furred hat. There were penalties for sartorial mistakes, such as reversing the colours of a parti-coloured suit, and an Alderman of Walbrook was fined a dinner to all his colleagues for appearing on Whit-Monday to ride with the Mayor without a lining to his cloak.

For royal occasions cloth of gold was hung out in Cheap and all the conduits ran wine. The mummeries and pageants were marvels of fantasy : after Agincourt Henry V was received with a tremendous show starting with a triumphal arch, symbolic figures, and a band of trumpets on the Bridge, and boys dressed as angels in a window singing the Agincourt hymn. In Cornhill there were massed prophets in golden mantles singing psalms, who let forth a cloud of sparrows and small birds which perched on the king and flew around him. In Cheap were dancing virgins, while more boys dressed as angels showered (imitation) gold coins on the king. Further on was a great glittering figure of the Sun under a canopy upheld by angels surmounted by a gold archangel, and around it danced more virgins who blew gold leaves at the king. When Henry died the citizens followed him to St. Paul's with torches, in dead silence, clothed in white.

III

THE fierce self-will of the two great Tudors, Henry VIII and Elizabeth was a chastening experience for the Londoners. The Dissolution made England an independent, national state, and the City of London and Westminster together as the capital, were regarded as a unity ; the City's monetary power was temporarily defeated by the device of raising loans in Antwerp. The Londoners accepted the Dissolution for reasons mainly secular; because Henry was determined, and because the foreigner in religion, as elsewhere, was an encroachment which they were delighted to shake off. As the Reformation gathered momentum, however, it seemed to re-inspire all the sturdy independence of the Londoners, and when the Stuart reigns began, London was a fiercely Protestant town, tending to Puritanism, as independent as ever.

With the spread of education London was developing among her merchants and craftsmen an educated middle class, with ability and seriousness which, it was remarked at the time, fitted them far better than the nobles and people about the Court, for the highest offices. Sir Thomas More, and Colet, founder of St. Paul's School which educated so many great Londoners, are types of the time and of a more adult mind than that

THE SOUTHWARK END OF OLD LONDON BRIDGE IN 1616
Detail from an engraving by J. Visscher

of the earlier Londoners. They were among the influences which sent Londoners thinking along new channels ; poor people could read too, and there was a revival of Lollardry and eager Bible-reading, which Colet's fiery sermons easily fanned to anti-clericalism. It was said of the Londoners that if they had had to try Cain they would have acquitted him if Abel had been a priest.

After heroic efforts to be loyal to Mary Tudor, horrified at the holocaust of citizens and shopkeepers in the Smithfield Fires, London turned eagerly to Elizabeth who was welcomed with ecstasy, and with the most elaborate and exhausting, probably, of all the City pageants. A truly royal mettle sustained her as she drove indefatigably from each fantastic tableau to the next, listening to anthems and orations, long-winded compliments and "pretty sentences," mostly in Latin, delivered by London's highly-trained school-children, and making at each point apt and painstaking replies. For once the Londoners were not disappointed in their sovereign. Her main principles, to oust foreigners from religion, politics, and trade, and to keep, as far as possible, independence and peace, were precisely their own. The Prayer Book and the Bible were restored, six great Bibles were set up in St. Paul's for all to read, there were Bibles in houses, even in taverns, and the mob rushed about London smashing and spoiling crosses and sculptures, the charming ornaments of their town.

21

One of Elizabeth's first acts was to send for Sir Thomas Gresham for his advice on improving the currency. This great Londoner, a Mercer, an adroit financier, was employed by the Crown to raise loans in Antwerp. He forced the rate of exchange up, that of interest down, smuggled arms out of Flanders to England, and gathered information about the intended invasion. Envious of the Antwerp *Bourse*, he built a *Bourse* in London, partly out of his own pocket, with the golden grasshopper, the badge of his house, upon a column. Elizabeth, at an impressive opening ceremony, christened it the Royal Exchange.

Gresham undoubtedly feathered his nest, indeed he had several, in Bishopsgate, at Osterley, at Mayfield, all richly furnished ; but he was a great public servant and he left his fortune and his London house for the foundation of Gresham College, where Dr. Blow taught music, and Wren eventually lectured on astronomy.

Elizabeth was arbitrary with monopolies and taxes, but she encouraged great trade ventures and the merchants' efforts to compete with the Spanish, the Portuguese and Dutch whom they found everywhere upon the seas before them. The Russia Company was founded and the "pale Muscovites, sea-sick from Muscovy" were warmly received in London. In 1590 the German Steelyard at last was closed. There was a momentary recalcitrance in the City when, at the sack of Antwerp, Elizabeth was obliged for the first time to ask the City for a loan. It was refused and Sir Thomas Gresham had to patch the matter up. But when invasion threatened, Elizabeth's firm demands for men, money and ships were generously met. When she died there was such a "sighing and weeping and groaning as the like hath not been seen or known in the memory of man."

As the times improved, the streets, as streets will, got more congested than ever, with wheeled traffic now, the draymen "oft asleep behind their horses," and "the world now went on wheels whose parents were content to go afoot." The river was a great by-pass, with forty thousand watermen shouting at the river steps. The trades were still in districts ; there was Goldsmith's Row in Cheap, "the most beautiful frame of fair houses" ; the mercers had moved to the Bridge, but fish as always was in Thames Street, and the brewers "remain faithful to the friendly water of Thames." The nave of St. Paul's was a promenade for strollers, "Paul's Walk," where ale and greenstuff could be bought, lawyers consulted, labour (including Bardolf) hired. There was a handsome ribbon-development along Holborn and beyond Bishopsgate, and a slummy one all the way to Limehouse. Whitechapel was choked with "little pestering cottages." Rich merchants had country seats at Stepney and Walthamstow, and would retire to the country when they had made their pile. The ruins of the old monasteries were very disfiguring, a foreigner said. Plague was frequent, sanitary rules were made but ignored. Thieves and rogues from everywhere congregated in slums outside the walls, the nucleus of the

SIR THOMAS GRESHAM
Lithograph after the oil painting by Antonio Mor, 1512-1575

future London mob ; and in schools for thieves little boys were taught
to pick money silently from purses hung with bells.

There was an exuberance of amusement, people ruined themselves
gaming and dicing. Bankside (the stews were adjacent) was uproarious
with bull- and bear-baiting and cock-fighting, which some thought cruel,
but not Elizabeth, who thought them "sweet and comfortable," keeping

23

the working class out of mischief on Sundays. Wrestling was a passion, and the second scene of *As You Like It* was performed with professional wrestlers. The fairs were popular as ever but beginning to be mocked by the sophisticated. In 1562 when the Thames froze over there was a fair on the ice, which became more crowded than any street.

Music was everywhere, from the solemn Masses of Byrd, to the importunate tavern entertainers. A gentleman was expected "to know no more than to sing a part sure, at first sight," and a party of merchants met daily in a house in Cornhill for the practice of music. Learning flourished, and antiquarianism ; John Stow sat among his musty books and manuscripts compiling his immortal record of the City's antiquities. Two new schools, Christ's Hospital and Merchant Taylors', replaced those lost in the Dissolution, and Westminster School was refounded.

The great flood of Elizabethan literature had its source in London, with Spenser, a Londoner born. Poetry, novelettes, pamphlets, poured from the printing presses to meet the endless demand for books. Printers would pay Greene dear "for the very dregs of his wit." Most sensational was the burst of drama ; though partly of the court with its masques and revels, it had a more human foundation in the heart of London. Nash, Peele, Greene, Kyd, in poverty, tipplers in taverns, struck off the first great English plays, followed close by Marlowe, Shakespeare, Beaumont, Fletcher, Ben Jonson. Few of these were Londoners born, but London made them, they drew their inspiration from its streets, its taverns and the life they found there.

Like the rest of England, London had run mad for plays, and the City, increasingly puritanical, fearing the spread of plague in the crowded audiences, accidents from stage effects, and dangers to the morals of the maidens, condemned the players to be licensed and the plays to be read by Aldermen before performance. So the plays went to the suburbs, to the "Curtain" and the "Theatre" at Shoreditch, and to Bankside, where, in theatres which have become immortal, eating apples and oranges, smoking and spitting, roaring applause or throwing rotten eggs, the Londoner might see the first performance on any stage of *Everyman in his Humour, Romeo and Juliet*, *King Lear*, or *Hamlet*, *Prince of Denmark*, with William Shakespeare as the ghost.

IV

THE seventeenth century, from the death of Elizabeth, to the accession of Anne, saw a tremendous constitutional struggle, combined with a religious conflict, in which the Londoners took a decisive part.

They had accepted Elizabeth's absolutism for its compensating benefits ; the Stuarts brought a period of tyranny, extortion and pandering to

FIRE IN LONDON

Coloured aquatint by Pugin and Rowlandson

From *The Microcosm of London*. Ackermann, 1808

By courtesy of the Guildhall Library, London

THE FUNERAL OF THE DUKE OF WELLINGTON IN 1852

Coloured lithograph by T. Picken after Louis Haghe

"Popery" and foreigners, a reversal of everything for which London had always striven. London returned to its old independent attitude, and defied the Stuarts as it had defied the Plantagenets, even to the bitterness of civil war.

James I's reign began well with superb coronation pageantry in the City, and bonfires for the Gunpowder Plot. But soon followed disillusionment in the execution of Raleigh and other panderings to Spain. When the projected Spanish Marriage fell through, there were bonfires and tables spread for feasting in the streets. Sabbatarian London would not even amuse itself on Sundays to please James; the city clergy preferred to pay fines rather than read out the Book of Sports which he issued to encourage reasonable exercise on the working man's only free day. The royal carriages were even refused passage in the City, and when James threatened to leave London the Lord Mayor made his famous retort that it did not signify where he went if he left the Thames behind him.

With Charles I relations were bad almost from the start. When he dissolved Parliament and immediately asked the City for £10,000, many of the citizens went to prison rather than pay. Everything that Parliament did to thwart Charles was celebrated with bonfires in the City. There was indirect as well as direct extortion. Building was prohibited outside the City in order to compel the suburban householders to ransom their houses by payment of three years' rent in lieu of demolition. Prynne and his fellow pamphleteers were greeted as martyrs and when Ship-money was demanded, the King got a list of grievances instead. There were riots against the Spanish Embassy, against Laud, and shouts of joy on Tower Hill when Strafford's head fell. When Charles at last fled from London it was in terror of the angry crowds parading at Whitehall headed by the apprentices with their cropped hair, called "Roundheads" by the Court.

When Charles raised his standard at Nottingham troops and money were instantly forthcoming to oppose him; the Companies and citizens melted down their plate. There was a moment of panic after Edgehill, but the City trainbands turned the King's forces back at Turnham Green. Earthworks were ordered to be thrown up round the City (few were actually dug), and when Gloucester was besieged the trainbands marched across England to relieve it. As the war went badly for the Parliament Londoners had misgivings; they had intended a swift stroke to frighten Charles to his senses, not a long, bitter war. Trade was dead; there were bankruptcies, and the citizens' wives demonstrated at Westminster for peace. Naseby restored confidence, and when the Long Parliament went Presbyterian the ruling class in London was with it despite the numerous sectaries led by "cobblers, tailors and the like" of which London was the headquarters. But when the army was not disbanded, and a second civil war threatened, London almost rose for Charles. Fairfax, however, occupied London and

Cromwell was accepted, philosophically rather than with conviction, with feasting and presents of gold plate. But the Lord Mayor refused to proclaim the abolition of monarchy and three out of the five aldermen appointed to try Charles refused to serve.

The Commonwealth brought peace, but between the abolition of all plays and sports in 1653, and the dissolution of Parliament in 1654, London began to recover from extreme Puritanism and to think better of kings. When the army deposed Richard Cromwell and recalled the Rump parliament, the people in the streets, the sailors on the river, were all shouting for a free parliament. Soon the Royal Arms appeared on Skinners' Hall, and *EXIT TYRANNUS REGUM ULTIMUS* quietly vanished from the Royal Exchange. There was frenzied joy at the Restoration, with bonfires and drinking (too much, Pepys thought), and rumps of beef roasted in the streets with flames leaping to the overhanging casements, while the butchers rang tattoos with their knives. The coronation pageantry in the city was a blaze of black velvet, white satin, cloth of silver, gold chains, and superb horses.

Charles II, like most of his predecessors, was a disappointment to London. The ancient charters were confirmed, but the Act of Uniformity dispossessed many of the sermon-loving City's most respected divines. The Plague of 1665 and the Fire of the next year were judgments of Providence to be sustained with fortitude ; far more galling was the feeble conduct of the Dutch war, the Dutch in the Medway, and the (then unfamiliar) sound of guns in the City. There were the usual difficulties about money, and when Charles closed the Exchequer where the Goldsmiths, who acted as bankers, kept their deposits, many business people were ruined. The City ranged itself against the succession of the Catholic Duke of York, and Charles, exasperated, took away the City's charters, the cherished heritage bought and extorted from all the kings of England through the centuries. The humiliation was severe, but the Londoners had to put up with it, as with the persecution of Dissenters, and the unblushing way of life at Court. They called the Court a brothel, but left it at that. After all, they had tried Puritan rule, and an alternative to monarchy, and felt disinclined for further experiment.

James II's open encouragement of "Popery" and of foreigners, the public floggings and the burning at Tyburn of a quiet old lady, a Baptist, who sheltered someone suspected of complicity in the Rye House Plot, were unpleasant shocks for Londoners. People walked out of church when the Declaration of Indulgence was read, and when the seven bishops who petitioned against it were taken to the Tower, kneeling crowds demanded their blessing. When the news of their acquittal spread, there were tears of joy, and from the crowds in the streets, the ships in the Thames, even from the sophisticated people in the Coffee-houses, the cheering rolled through all London from Westminster to the Tower. At night there

26

"The True Maner of the Execution of Thomas Earle of Strafford upon Tower Hill
12th May 1641"
Engraving by W. Hollar, 1607-1677

were bonfires, rockets, squibs, candles in every window. When James
fled, the invitation to William of Orange was dated from the Guildhall,
by the Peers, the Aldermen and Common Council. The coronation was
dazzling with illuminations and fireworks, orange streamers in the theatres,
and people paraded the streets like Dutchmen with oranges on sticks.

These vicissitudes brought no check to London's intellectual life,
rather they seemed to stimulate it. Elizabethan literature had poured
its full torrent almost to the eve of the Civil War, taking a more sombre
colour with Donne's passionate verses and sermons at the Deanery of
St. Paul's. Palladian architecture and town-planning began with Inigo
Jones's Lincoln's Inn Fields, and the Piazza at Covent Garden. Early in
the century Bacon, discredited as Lord Chancellor, turned to science
with his *Novum Organum*, and Harvey was lecturing on the circulation of
the blood. When the troubles had subsided, almost immediately a great
age began, greater, for London, than any before it. Poetry was carried
over the bleak years of the Commonwealth, raised in fact to entirely new
eminences by Milton, sometimes called the greatest Londoner of all.
Paradise Lost was published five years after the Restoration in the London
of Dryden and the Coffee-houses, of Restoration drama, of Lely's pictures,
the Athenian London of Evelyn, Pepys, and Wren. In 1662 the Royal
Society was formed by a group of people, formerly centred upon Gresham

27

College, who had continued their scientific researches in private under the Commonwealth, for "to be ever musing upon public distresses were too melancholy a reflection." Music too, though it had flourished in private life after its banishment from the churches, flowered afresh as Pepys has shown us, and in 1672 the first concerts to be given for money anywhere were held by Banister, a London violinist, at his house in Whitefriars, with sometimes "a parley of instruments" by eminent masters. A little later, Britton the Clerkenwell charcoal hawker, held subscription concerts over his coal store with an organ of five stops, on which Handel eventually played, and virginals said to be the best in Europe.

The Coffee-houses, a London invention, were the great innovation of the age. The earliest was the *Turk's Head* in St. Michael's Alley, Cornhill, opened in 1652. They focussed fashionable, literary and political life and were centres of news, gossip and free discussions. There were other drinks besides coffee and, except at the most foppish houses, clouds of tobacco smoke. A tobacconist died in 1688 worth £300,000. They became for the time "the Londoner's home : those who wished to find a gentleman asked, not where he lived, but whether he frequented the *Rainbow* or the *Grecian*." Each house gathered its particular clique : at *Will's*, which was for poets and wits, Dryden presided ; the *St. James's* was Whig ; the *Cocoa Tree* Tory ; *Man's* and *Young Man's* near Whitehall for stock-jobbers, sharpers and fops ; *Tomkyn's* and the *Rose* at Covent Garden for rakes and "gentlemen to whom beds are unknown" ; and there were many more. Doctors were consulted in them and business done : *Jonathan's* in 'Change Alley became the Stock Exchange, *Lloyd's* became Lloyd's as we know it. In the political houses talk was so free that Charles II, in alarm, tried to close them, but the order could not be enforced.

Taverns were not in abeyance : Pepys visited a hundred and twenty eight in the course of his day-to-day rambles, and there were celebrated eating-houses such as Pontack's in the city, where dinner was from £1 1s. to £2 2s., patronised by the Royal Society in its early years.

The Restoration brought a joyous resumption of almost all the old sports. Both Evelyn and Pepys (rather ashamed of themselves) saw great bull-baiting at the Bear Garden. Cocks were the rage : at a cockpit in Shoe Lane, Pepys saw "people who look as if they had not bread to put in their mouths betting three or four pounds, losing and betting as much again." Stakes were enormous : in St. James's Park Evelyn saw a wrestling match with £1,000 laid, and fighting was everywhere, most democratically, between people of different rank, and there was football "even in Crooked Lane."

The pleasure gardens began their great vogue with the old Spring Gardens near the Mall, dull and expensive, Pepys said, full of gallantry according to Tom Brown, and the Mulberry Garden, with much love-making, late hours, and a famous Spanish cook. Across the river, New

28

Spring Gardens, later known as Vauxhall, made a tentative start. The old fairs flourished despite ridicule and in 1683 there was a tremendous Ice Fair, by no means the last, upon the Thames.

By 1660 several theatres were re-opened and crowded, "prentices and mean people" who would formerly pay only 1/- for the pit now crowded it at 2/6. The mobbing for seats was frightful, a foreigner remarked, and Pepys saw a thousand people turned away from *She Would if She Could*. Audiences were noisy and sociable, and women now took women's parts, an improvement much relished by Pepys. At Killigrew's new theatre at Drury Lane, Nell Gwyn and the "Orange Molls" bandied backchat with the gallants during the performance. People were soon tired of the old plays (Pepys thought the *Dream* mighty insipid) and the sparkling, dirty Restoration playwrights came to the rescue, with their easy modern dialogue, poking fun at everybody's foibles.

Mayoral pageantry was of undimmed splendour throughout the century. Even under the Commonwealth there had been modest shows with Temperance and the Virtues, giants, griffins, Pan and satyrs. For Anne's accession a Vintner Lord Mayor sponsored a splendid affair with Ariadne in a car drawn by panthers. But sophisticated people looked down on these old-fashioned pomposities, though the common people loved them as ever. It is said that they never quite recovered from the postponement occasioned by the death of Anne's Prince Consort in 1708. In 1711 the Lord Mayor at his "triumph" fell off his horse, since when he has journeyed to Westminster more prudently by coach.

Fun and fashion were moving westwards, splendid squares, St. James's, Berkeley, Soho, took their shape after the Restoration. Even in the city there were many houses of the merchants panelled and with painted ceilings, while the ladies' nests were lined with feathers and ribbons, though they were not often in them, being fonder of gadding abroad in their coaches or sedans (the latter more expeditious as taking up less of the narrow ways). Hyde Park was a great meeting-place for people in their coaches, and St. James's Park and the Mall for strolling, gazing and gallant encounters. There was much shopping for ribbons, fans, gloves and toys in the booths at the Royal Exchange and at the 'New Change' in the Strand, and the pretty shop-girls lisped distractingly and played shuttle-cock between whiles. There were shady spots in the "Rookery" in St. Giles's, Whetstone Park, Lewknor's Lane, and the old sanctuaries at Westminster and White-friars ; and the mob (porters and odd-jobbers living in the slums south of Holborn) was becoming an institution. There were highwaymen, pickpockets, horse-thieves, unchecked by the extreme feebleness of the watch. Heming's modest little lamps at every tenth house-door, on one night in three, from six to twelve, moonless nights only, gave rise to as much controversy as Willett's daylight-saving, but made some improvement in public safety. The river was a scene of great beauty, the

29

Pool so packed with shipping that only a narrow channel remained for navigation. The watermen had a bad reputation for obscenity and foul backchat; the dockers on the other hand, Ticket-Porters they were called, were extremely respectable and took Holy Communion at a special annual service at St. Mary-at-Hill, with nosegays in their hands.

Across all the fun, politics, and philosophy, the Plague and the Fire cut a hideous gash. Plagues and fires were familiar, but these surpassed all. In the plague, people's behaviour was of all kinds : those who could find a refuge fled, many of them having no call to remain. Many remained, doctors, city officials, constables, churchwardens, all attended to their often grim and dangerous duties, good women nursed the stricken, important people bustled stoically about their business. "You, sir," Pepys wrote to Sir William Coventry, "took your turn of the sword; I must not grudge mine of the pestilence." The Lord Mayor and the Aldermen made what sanitary rules they could, and sat daily to give help and advice. The poor showed a very "Turkish predestinarianism," in contempt of infection. Some sat in such taverns as were open hoping to meet their end drinking. There were the Londoners' customary graveyard jokes, and there was a great friendliness, "people were no longer shy of one another." Even Dissenting and Episcopal congregations and clergy forgot their quarrels and mixed freely at worship.

At the first sign of abatement people came crowding back (the mortality figures went up again for a time), there was a great whitewashing and cleansing, and soon London seemed as populous as before.

THE GREAT PLAGUE, 1665
Engraving by N. Sherlock after S. Wale

30

OLD ST. PAUL'S ON FIRE
Engraving by Wenceslaus Hollar, 1607-1677

When the Fire began (in the baker's shop in Pudding Lane), there was, for a few hours, a sort of paralysis of shock. The Lord Mayor refused at first to take the outbreak seriously (he was a man of "very silly conversation," Pepys said) but soon, though already too late, water was strenuously plied and houses were torn down in the path of the blaze which was driven by a high east wind. A seaman early suggested blowing up houses, but this the Lord Mayor refused to do without permission of the owners, many of whom, wealthy merchants and aldermen, were out of town for the weekend, leaving their town premises locked up untenanted. The poorer people worked indefatigably to quench the flames, but nothing availed till the King and the Duke of York, in fear for Whitehall, gave orders for charges of gunpowder, and eventually the wind changed. There was a not very dignified helter-skelter of citizens to save their goods in carts and lighters, but when the fire had such a hold, there was little else to be done, and in those days people's wealth was to a great extent stored in goods and chattels at their houses and business premises.

Everyone seemed to expect that after two such disasters the Londoners would be cast down. Not at all. After the Plague, there had been "the same cheerfulness of mind as before," and the second calamity says Dr. Sprat, Bishop of Rochester, "they endured with such firmness of mind that we may believe that the best moral philosophy may be learned from

31

the shops of Mechanics . . . no unmanly Bewailings were heard . . . not the least pusillanimity . . . Among their horrible ruins they prosecuted the war with the same vigour and courage against three of the most powerful states in Europe." Within about four years, London was raised again and everything seemed as flourishing as before.

The Londoner's power of recuperation was almost excessive. A few days before the Fire, a commission which included Evelyn and Wren, for the repair of St. Paul's, was plumbing and measuring and debating what should be done. A few days later the Fire removed all grounds of difference, including St. Paul's and five-sixths of the City, giving Wren's genius the opportunity to replace the old crooked, cramped, plague-ridden London by a city of dreams. Pepys feared that during the deliberations the precipitate Londoner would rebuild it "by fits," piecemeal; and so it was. The flames had but just died when people were back again, camping upon their plot to protect it from commissions and planners. Swift rebuilding of London was Wren's tragedy, and Wren's dome and Wren's towers were to rise above streets hardly less confused and congested than before.

V

WITH the age of Anne, not without its tempests (the Duke of Marlborough's wars, the Duchess of Marlborough's own particular wars, the wars of Whig and Tory, of High Church and Dissenters) the City settled down to immense prosperity and much less direct action in politics than before. Financial relations with the government became less personal, though no less intimate, with the foundation of the Bank of England and the establishment of the National Debt, both of which secured the City's antipathy to the Stuart Pretenders, whose probable way with money and debts was easy to imagine. The East India Company had outmatched the Dutch in the East, other companies expanded and the Royal Exchange was "buzzing with a noise like bees, a kind of roaring or loud whisper." Huge fortunes were piled up in the City, in a highly adventurous spirit which led to a fever of speculation in the South Sea Bubble of 1720 in which everyone was involved, and white faces in the City when the shares fell in a month from 800 to 189. The City's jealousy of its privileges flared up afresh when the Admiralty dared to send press officers into the City, and in the commotions about Wilkes and his printers, whom the City chose to champion as martyrs to the cause of a free press, disputing their arrests as illegal without signature of the City magistrates.

The intellectual life of London passed from the seventeenth to the eighteenth century without a pause. Wren was Surveyor General till 1718 and Newton was Master of the Mint. The scene shifts swiftly to the

By courtesy of the Artist

BANK HOLIDAY AT THE ZOO

Oil painting by S. van Abbé

By courtesy of the Artist

COVENT GARDEN MARKET

Oil painting by Hilda Davis

Augustan age, with its new literary constellation, Pope, Gray, Addison, Steele, Gay, and the startling outburst of Hogarth's miraculous painting. The Coffee-houses were talking and scintillating more than ever, and there were some new ones, *Button's*, where Addison presided, *White's*, celebrated for gaming, and *Old Slaughter*, where Hogarth was to be found. Society was raffish and gay, but there was a reaction towards morals ; in the *Tatler* and *Spectator*, Steele and Addison tried to rescue brightness from dirt. No place on earth, Voltaire said, was so much interested in literature. There was not much religion ; in the security of the Test Act the Church had become very flat and dull, and Dissent was rather stagnant too, till the emotional preaching of Whitefield and the Wesleys, with their Love Feasts in Fetter Lane and preaching at the Foundry at Moorfields, woke up religious feeling. No human age has been so minutely recorded, in letters, essays, poems, novels, and none other has had a Hogarth, born, bred, living wholly in London, to paint with intimate knowledge and dazzling technique (and perhaps an excess of spleen) the social character of his town. Horace Walpole dining, gossiping, letter-writing, seems to focus and link up nearly everyone in the century.

Hard on the heels of the Augustans follows Hanoverian London, glittering with high lights, Dr. Johnson, Sir Joshua Reynolds, Goldsmith, Sheridan, Gibbon ; the novel is launched by Richardson, the printer of Salisbury Square, and Fielding, and passes to Fanny Burney, and at the theatre there are Garrick and the Cibbers, Kitty Clive, Peg Woffington and eventually Siddons. The Royal Academy was founded in 1768 with Reynolds as first President, and from the depths of Saxony stout, irritable, sublime, Handel descended on the British people, bestowing upon them the *Fire*, the *Water* and other indispensable musics, and something which they have always regarded as among the foremost of their many blessings, the *Messiah*.

As the century advanced the Coffee-houses lost ground and the taverns reasserted themselves. Reynold's "Club," founded to give Dr. Johnson "unlimited opportunities for talking," met at the *Turk's Head* in Gerrard Street ; the *Devil* and the *Mitre*, Fleet Street, old haunts of the Muses, now saw Reynolds playing whist with Goldsmith, and Johnson sitting up all night with Mrs. Lennox, to celebrate her first novel. Gradually the clubs left the public taverns and coffee-houses and became *White's* and *Boodle's* and *Brooks's*. Female clubs met in the member's salons. The *Blue Stocking* struck awe among the opposite sex—or most of them : "Dearest you're a dunce," said Dr. Johnson to Miss Monckton when she pretended to have found Sterne's writings pathetic.

Interest in everything artistic was passionate ; the Royal Academy arose from a split in the Society of Artists, there were brawls and feuds about the respective merits of Italian *prime donne* (costly canary-birds, Cibber called them) and even in the Abbey over rival performers in the

33

Messiah. The *Beggar's Opera* and Arne maintained the English tradition in music, but foreign music was the rage. "I have had a shock," wrote Leopold Mozart, at taking 100 guineas in three hours. Haydn had an overwhelming reception—and too many dinners. There were various concerts : the Academy of Ancient Music which tried to hold out against Handel, the Castle Concerts at the *Castle* in Paternoster Row and the Handel-worshipping Concerts of Ancient Music, where J. C. Bach played, (with George II and later Prince Albert as Directors) and at the end of the century the Professional and the Salomon Concerts, especially devoted to Haydn. There were glees and choirs ; the Gentlemen's and Noble-men's Catch Club was presided over by George IV as Prince of Wales, and is still the City Glee Club. Artistic passions rent the theatres too. To raise prices was to evoke tempests : in 1763 the O.P. (Old Prices) Riots wrecked the interiors of Covent Garden theatre and Drury Lane.

The twin foci of fun and fashion were Vauxhall and Ranelagh, with their classic-romantic groves, grottoes, rotundoes, temples, passionately enjoyed by everyone. At Vauxhall the entrance was a shilling and everyone was there "from the Duke of Grafton to the children of the Foundling Hospital," including the City folk ("Cits" the smart world called them) and people could bring their food, as at the famous supper-party where Walpole and Lady Petersham minced seven chickens in a china chafing-dish with everyone looking on, "stirring and rattling and laughing and expecting the dish every minute to fly about our ears." There was tea and coffee and bread-and-butter and ham cut so thin you could read the paper through it. The illuminations were fairy-like, (human) nightingales warbled from the trees, and there were concerts of Handel and Arne. Ranelagh pretended to greater elegance with orange trees with lights in the oranges, auriculas and festoons of real flowers. Here little Mozart played a concerto on the organ in aid of the Lying-in-Hospital ("that is one way," said Leopold Mozart, "of winning the affections of this exceptional people") or Dr. Burney might provide some light music for the "salt-box, cleavers, hum-strum, and hurdy-gurdy." All over London the less pretentious pleasure gardens and "spas," Marylebone Gardens, Barnigge Wells, Islington Spa, Sadler's Wells, Hampstead, and less respectably, Cuper's Gardens in Bermondsey, Finch's Grotto, Lambeth Gardens, the Dog and Duck (where Bethlehem Hospital now stands), gathered their thousands, both fashion and the "Cits." The Pantheon was a winter resort with "Handel Nights," ("who can have a manner who has not seen the Pantheon?"). Almack's, founded in 1765, a "female Club," strikes a new note of exclusiveness.

There were the old vulgar amusements ; bears and bulls had sunk in the social scale, cocks had risen, and the betting on everything—races of old women, anything—was tremendous. Southwark Fair had a great vogue. Streets were lively with pugilism, football (the balls bouncing everywhere), as well as street-cries, ballad singers, herds of cattle, pick-

THE ENRAGED MUSICIAN
Engraving after William Hogarth, 1697-1764

pockets, wig-snatchers, and congested to curses with drays, coaches and
sedans. People must know when to take the wall and when to give it, to
avoid a fight. A foreigner on the other hand remarked upon the convenience
and urbanity of the London streets : there were "more people abroad
at midnight in London than in many continental cities at mid-day," and
there was a remarkable equality—all classes mixed and jostled freely.
St. James's Park the people had made peculiarly their own, in fact "they
were sovereign in the streets."

The mob had too much "sovereignty" in fact and had become, as
Fielding said, a fourth estate. Soaked in gin (reputed to have been intro-
duced by William III), sold, despite the Gin Acts, at a few pence the pint,
some at least were reducing themselves to the state depicted in Hogarth's
Gin Lane. They would rush out at any political cry, for Wilkes, or against
"Popery" as in the Gordon Riots of 1780, when they set a distillery on

35

A SELLER OF HAIR BROOMS
Engraving after Craig, 1804

fire, burned themselves, and almost burned London. As for the High-Life terrors, the Mohock, the Hell-Fire Clubs, whether they really slit noses, overturned sedans and rolled women in tubs, or were merely a form of bogeyism, seems to be in doubt.

Social life was creeping west of Temple Bar : "the full tide," Johnson said, "is at Charing Cross." Hanover and Cavendish Squares had superseded Leicester Fields and Lincoln's Inn Fields. The river was still the main thoroughfare, but there were two new bridges, Westminster and Blackfriars. Eastwards was another world and "the further you go eastwards the more domestic does life become." The "Cits" lived among and over their shops in the City (it was a social slur to live there), keeping up the old sermon-loving respectability combined, in the English way, with a passion for amusements. They flocked to Vauxhall, Ranelagh and all the less modish gardens, and the ladies sighed for coaches, servants and titled acquaintance. They were Dissenters, and Evangelicals ; according to a German, Sunday was all cold meat and hymns, and he was rebuked by his landlady's child for singing. An American, however, found the number of Sunday amusements "inconceivable." The well-to-do merchants tended to live out at Stepney, Stoke Newington, Streatham (where the Thrales lived), at "Evangelical" Hackney, where a hundred families had their coach, and at Clapham, which gave birth to the Clapham Sect and the Bible Society. The riverside life from the Tower to Ratcliffe had a sinister reputation, but Boswell, sent by Johnson to explore it, was "much disappointed." About the genuine working class no one knew or thought much, watchmakers in Clerkenwell, weavers in Spitalfields, Bethnal Green, Mile End, and innumerable trades in the villages north and east. They were poor, sober, industrious. After the Fire of 1666,

36

the city was given up to the commercial classes, business, and merchandise, while the craftsmen were in the growing villages without the city boundaries. They were a natural soil for the radicalism of the latter part of the century, and London was the headquarters of the Corresponding Society, the leaders of which, in the panic following the September massacres in Paris in 1792, were tried for their lives, but acquitted. The London artisans however, with their diverse small industries carried on in their homes, received the Industrial Revolution slowly and without upheaval. Gin was not their foible; they drank ale, and like the rest of England were betaking themselves to a nice cup of tea.

London of the eighteenth century was a mixture of humanitarianism and cruelty. People lay starved to death in deserted tenements. Bedlam and the prisons were heart-rending; hangings at Tyburn were public holidays with gin sold in the crowd for refreshment. Heads, till 1776, rotted on Temple Bar with spy-glasses hired out to look at them. But nearly all the great London hospitals were founded in the middle of the century, including the Foundling Hospital, with Hogarth on the Board, and Handel playing the organ and conducting the *Messiah*.

VI

AMID the heart-searchings caused by the French Revolution and the Napoleonic Wars, the gay life of the Regency and of the reign of George IV seems like a hangover from the dissipations of the eighteenth century. The round of fun, fighting, cocks, bets, routs, operas, tarts, assemblies was trodden industriously and can be followed in Rowlandson's and other cartoons of the time, and in the Adventures of *Tom and Jerry*. Snobbery and exclusiveness were increasing; Almack's was paramount, ruled by its ten great patronesses, Lady Jersey, the future Lady Palmerston, and the rest, who once refused Wellington admission when he arrived after 11 p.m. The clubs and the great political houses focussed the intellectual, political and fashionable worlds; Devonshire House for the Tories, Holland House for the Whigs, where Sydney Smith, Samuel Rogers, Scott, Byron, Tom Moore were to be found. At Gore House Lady Blessington and the beautiful (and insolvent) Count d'Orsay entertained everybody, respectable and other, in the first decade of Victoria's reign. The Regency tradition was carried on by the Swell Mob in the new reign, followed by the Snobs, driven by sheer boredom to eccentricity, till even they were borne down by the rising middle class, invading with the power of wealth, and of talent, many strongholds hitherto closed to them. At the close of the century the Regency tradition, for it seems to be a permanent element in London life, flowered again in the

37

COVENT GARDEN THEATRE, 1795
Water colour by Edward Dayes

"naughty nineties" and was far from extinct in the twentieth (prior, that is to say, to 1939).

The early years of the century were not without inventions. In 1828 the Zoo began, in 1829 the Police. A great page was turned in scientific discovery with Faraday's experiments in electricity at the Royal Institution.

Pageantry still flourished. For the peace celebrations in 1814 the Green Park had a castle for fireworks, while St. James's Park went Chinese, with a willow-pattern bridge over the water, a pagoda from which rockets made a pillar of fire, and Chinese lanterns everywhere; Hyde Park fought Trafalgar all over again with a brilliant nocturnal *Naumachia* on the Serpentine.

As for the City it feasted the Prince Regent, the Czar, the King of Prussia, Blücher and a cloud of Field-Marshals, Serene Highnesses and foreign exaltednesses, at a banquet which seemed the climax of the City's gustatory history. Even the waiters were "gentlemen of respectability." The Lord Mayor and Aldermen dashingly mounted beribboned chargers to meet and escort the guests.

There were three coronations in twenty years; the finest, that of George IV, was rendered piquant by the divorced Queen's unsuccessful effort to be crowned.

38

THE ROYAL BANQUET GIVEN TO HER MAJESTY QUEEN VICTORIA BY THE CORPORATION
OF LONDON
The Guildhall, Lord Mayor's Day, 9th November, 1837
Coloured aquatint by Thomas Dighton

The nineteenth century was as rich as any other in great Londoners, born and bred, as usual, in the most unpretentious homes; the sequence carries over without pause from the eighteenth century, with several people who seem already in the nineteenth, long before the blaze of the Johnsonian era was spent. Jeremy Bentham was born in the middle of the eighteenth century and Mary Wolstonecraft, among other early Radicals (to be joined later by William Godwin from the Hoxton Nonconformist Academy), and in the later decades Blake, Charles Lamb, Turner, Leigh Hunt, Byron, Keats, Thomas Hood. The great cartoonists, Rowlandson, Gillray, and later the Cruikshanks, have left pictures of the times, Hogarthian in their completeness, and sometimes their spleen. Literature was more important than ever, and publishers became potentates. In the second decade of the nineteenth century Thackeray and Dickens were born within a year of each other (Dickens came to London when he was two); essential Londoners themselves, creators of immortal Londoners. Close upon them follow John Stuart Mill, Ruskin, Browning, Disraeli; and Chelsea became a home of the Muses, with Carlyle and the Pre-Raphaelites, and then Whistler (a stranger but a good Londoner) and Wilde. The Press began to occupy its throne, and great correspondents appear, such as Sala. In the 'seventies the Royal Academy was enjoying a prestige almost equal to its early glories and Du Maurier's swan-like beauties swam to the Private View and the Drawing Rooms. Towards the close of the century Putney was sacred to Swinburne.

The Georges had been good music patrons and industrious performers, and concerts multiplied from the foundation of the Philharmonic Society in 1813, with the Sacred Harmonic Society, the Exeter Hall concerts for oratorios. (People fought for places at the Haymarket to hear Jenny Lind, and the Exeter Hall nearly had a riot when Mme. Novello refused an encore in the *Messiah*); then Crosby Hall, and the Crystal Palace and the *Pops* at the St. James's Hall (succeeded by our own *Proms*.). Foreign musicians continued to reap harvests—Mendelssohn, Weber, Liszt. Italian opera, so much in vogue under the musical young queen, gave way, alas, to Wagner, but English opera found a new voice with Gilbert and Sullivan at the Savoy.

From the beginning of the century there was great building : Nash's charming façades, new bridges, Trafalgar Square, Nelson's Column, the National Gallery, the British Museum ; London had a University College, and the Thames the Brunels' tunnel, and a long series of other improvements, moral, monumental and intellectual, followed. Prison reform had begun earlier :

"Oh Mrs. Fry, why go to Newgate, why,
Unless you make their betters better, fie."

Immense commercial prosperity, occasionally diversified with over-speculation, sent the City men's families to Kensington and Bayswater,

By courtesy of the Artist

THE ROW IN SPRING
Riding in Hyde Park
Oil painting by Beryl Sinclair

By courtesy of the Artist

'IT HAPPENED TO US'
Daylight raid on London, 1941
Oil painting by Carel Weight

where the female part forgot all about the City and its mysterious businesses, while lesser folk and clerks went out to Streatham, Camberwell, Stockwell, Camden Town, taking (to the surprise of their betters) to gardening, whence they went to the City by omnibus if they could afford it, if not, on foot. With the arrival of the Metropolitan railway in 1863 the great exodus from the City began in earnest till it became a city of half a million by day, of a bare ten thousand at night.

Behind all the wealth and culture was a background of grievous civic negligence and slums. Between 1750 and 1850 the population of London rose from under a million to over two. From Hammersmith to Limehouse, and north and south of the river, the old villages had spread out to meet one another, and eventually the railways set their heavy feet over the dull little streets built by speculators for the working people, adding smuts and grime to poverty. In the old central London slums there was filth, and air so foul, in places, from forgotten drains and cesspools, that tulips sickened and died. The old graveyards in and around the City—especially St. Andrew's, Holborn, and St. Bride's, were a noisome, gruesome horror. There were repeated outbreaks of cholera, and in 1836 the Directors of the Bank of England were startled to see a man appear suddenly in the middle of the floor in the bullion room at the Bank, having walked by an old sewer from Dowgate.

London was a wen, indeed, as Cobbett called it. Excepted from the Municipal Government Act of 1836, it was but an agglomeration of parishes grouped round the City, which, unlike other boroughs, had failed to extend with its population. Self-sufficing, cherishing its ancient traditions and prestige, the City ignored what lay outside its wards. The Metropolitan Board of Works, established in 1857, began to set about such matters as drainage ; but London had to wait till 1889 for the London County Council to bring order and coherence into chaos, and a prospect of reasonable corporate life.

As the London workman suffered less than the rest of England from the Industrial Revolution, so also, with his diversity of industries, he escaped the worst of the unemployment following the Napoleonic Wars, and there was little unrest in the early part of the century. Even the mob seemed calmer if not extinct, owing perhaps to the police, or more tea and less gin. The Chartist movement founded in London moved its headquarters to Birmingham. But wages and conditions in London were appalling and in the middle of the century dockers fought for work at the dock gates, and were paid fourpence an hour when they got it. Cranes were driven by men treading in wooden cylinders.

The contrast between rich and poor, Disraeli's "two nations," eventually disturbed the complacency of the prosperous Londoner. With the repeal of the Corn Laws, and the Shaftesbury Factory Acts came movements to cleanse, feed, uplift, study the poor, even to educate them. The early

41

THE CRYSTAL PALACE
Nineteenth Century lithograph by Vincent Brooks

career of *Punch* was devoted to the London poor, and when the 1851
Exhibition was in preparation, showed workers in rags as exhibits under
glass shades. The London City Mission, the cholera, and Dickens's
novels, have been called the three great agencies of social reform, to
which should be added Hood's *Song of a Shirt*. From the middle of the
century there was much effort to cope with London slum life, the Salvation
Army, the Christian Socialists with F. D. Maurice and Charles Kingsley,
Housing Reform, with Octavia Hill, the Charity Organisation Society
(with a tendency to insist on virtue in the poor), Settlements, devoted
self-sacrificing clergy, missionaries, "slumming" of many kinds. But
nothing seemed to catch up with the conditions, becoming inveterate with
the accretion of Irish labourers, and Jewish refugees from pogroms abroad.
Only trade organisation, helped, it must be admitted, by strikes, could
mend matters, and eventually social legislation. Better days began with
the great dock strike of 1889, when most of London, led by the Lord
Mayor and Cardinal Manning, was on the side of the strikers.

Through all his vicissitudes the Londoner has been sustained by his
immense patience and good temper, by the compensations in the life
and movement of a great capital city, and his many amusements. If
ferment has occasionally been roused as in 1886 and 1887, it has died
quickly, and the sense of injustice has turned to an extremely reasonable

DESIGN FOR A STREET CROSSING BRIDGE
Nineteenth Century engraving

socialism.   The dreary middle years of the century abounded in amusements;
tea gardens, and taverns with entertainments (successors to Vauxhall and the
old pleasure gardens), such as the Eagle in the City Road (supposedly the
tavern in "Pop goes the Weasel") where thousands nightly saw Shakespeare,
ballets, operas, fireworks and balloons, and later Cremorne with tight-rope-
walking over the river, and Madame Poitevin ascending on a heifer in a
balloon.   There was always Brighton, Epping Forest and the Heath,
steamer trips to Margate and Ramsgate, the theatres (many more in poorer
London formerly, than now), pantomimes, the "Halls," melodramas, pano-
ramas, cosmoramas, dioramas, the Westminster Aquarium, Tussaud's, the
Zoo, the Crystal Palace with bands and much *Messiah*, Lord's, the Oval,
fights in gloves, or (surreptitiously at dead of night and in the small hours)
without, football, the Boat Race, Doggett's race, and the Londoner's day of
days—the Derby.   Towards the end of the century drink more and more
gave way to other, more innocent consolations, cycling, athletics, gardening,
and back-yard joys such as pigeon and rabbit-fancying.
    The beginning of the twentieth century seems to belong to the nine-
teenth; but from 1911 (to those who remember what went before) the
Londoner's life has improved almost beyond recognition.   There have
been two tremendous wars, but it cannot be disputed that the years
between the wars, despite a disastrous slump and much timidity by

43

authority, saw profound changes for the better, accompanied of course by unrest and discontent, inconvenient but reassuring signs of progressiveness.

Many new joys were added, cinemas, radios, motor-transport, dirt-track racing, football pools, League matches (and disputes), the Cup Final, and youngest and perhaps most beloved of all, dog-racing. Now with Shakespeare in Regent's Park, and recent park pleasures developed for "Holidays at Home," even the old pleasure gardens are having a new birth.

Whatever the Londoner's troubles, tastes or foibles may have been, they have not sapped his fundamental quality. He has been tried again in the second German war, and not found wanting.

VII

WHEN the war broke in September 1939, many Londoners evacuated voluntarily or under pressure from authority. The Londoner who stayed, groped through the "phoney war" acquiring Civil Defence lore, and wondering if it would ever be needed.

When France fell many, spoiling for a fight, almost rejoiced that the war was coming nearer. Boats and barges from the whole dock system, including the *Daffodil* and the *Eagles* of the Clacton trip, put out for the urgent and hazardous rescues of the Dunkirk beaches, and engineers and engine-hands from all dockland, (some had never been afloat before) rushed forward as volunteers to provide relief crews for the rescue ships working day and night.

The implications of the fall of France were not perhaps fully grasped, and there was a tendency to regard the battle of Britain, while it was being fought, as the world's transcendant sporting event. On September 7th, 1940, under a sky red with the fires at the docks, the battle of London began, intended to strike at the heart of Britain by bringing London to its knees. Intuitively, rather than consciously, the Londoner accepted the challenge, sustaining an ordeal unparalleled (for the first nine weeks till the attack on Coventry) in history, with a fighting spirit expressed in the most obstinate fortitude.

Shelter life began, rather confusedly at first, later with miracles of organisation, sanitary and alimentary, by authority, and the joys of communal life, so much appreciated that many have been loth to relinquish them when the need of shelter passed. Two-thirds of the Londoners of the central areas made use of no shelter of any kind, public or private, but slept at home, under tables, under stairs, or just in bed. Those who had responsibilities, to the whine of bombs and spatter of spent shell, carried on a diversity of tasks, men and women alike "taking not a blind bit of notice of what was falling all round them," driving ambulances,

"Derby Day" on Epsom Downs
Oil painting by Arthur Knighton-Hammond

driving and manning fire appliances, repairing gasometers sixty feet in the air with millions of cubic feet of gas beneath them, wading breast-high in flooded basements to damp fires under bombed boilers, performing surgical operations by hand-torch in buildings shaken by blast, rescuing people from shattered houses, or from a collapsed shop sliding down a slippery clay crater to a gas main alight at the bottom. Once when a volunteer "of slender build" was asked for, a London Home Guard, a tiny man, taking a saw with him crawled through a tunnel burrowed through debris and extricated a number of imprisoned people by sawing through a beam upon which the superstructure appeared to, but miraculously did not, rest. Such acts became commonplaces and still are when need arises. Those who had no definite duties, surprised each morning to be still alive (if indeed they were), reached their daily work sometime, somehow, if it took them three hours, and in the evening often stayed at work to "finish" even if the homeward journey had to be performed to the accompaniment of the next night's sirens or bombs.

45

A virtuosity in ingenuity was displayed in the punctual arrival of milk, newspapers and letters, over broken glass and craters at addresses that were little else, and in maintaining existence in battered houses with the remnants of household equipment. Like Pepys in the Fire, many a Londoner was constrained to make "an ugly meal, in a sad manner," but, unless bereaved or injured, he could, like Pepys, be "very merry over it."

Sport continued—with some police restrictions on attendances. In the 1940-41 season the Southern Regional Football League programme was played in its entirety. Games were occasionally postponed, but in the heavily-blitzed Millwall, New Cross, Charlton, West Ham United districts, not one match was abandoned. In 1941, 60,000 people saw the Cup Final—with a "noisy" night to follow. Dog-racing also suffered restriction of spectators to 25,000 as against a normal 90,000, and the "Classics" were not held. Bombs fell during racing, and for a time there was a rule that racing must stop during an alert. But there was such strong feeling against this that the rule was rescinded. "Bang goes my two bob," someone cried as the Tote was hit.

Every Londoner felt, that anything he did, or refrained from doing, that helped to keep the wheels of daily life revolving and the ordinary routine alive was a blow at Hitler, and he was right. The Blitz was meant to rattle the Londoner, to paralyse him into panic, and it failed; his endurance was not passive, but aggressive, a direct retort to his enemy. The Londoner fought the battle of London and won.

In the fighting forces the Londoner has always won glory especially in difficulties. In 1914-18 the London regiments seemed nearly always in the worst places : at Loos, at Gommecourt, at Delville wood, at Ypres.

In heroism, which has become, in the present war, an every-day story in all the armed forces, Londoners can scarcely claim pre-eminence. They have, at any rate, a high proportion of all the recent awards for distinguished conduct. An early V.C. of the war was awarded, posthumously, to Leading Seaman J. F. Mantle, aged 23, of Battersea, who, with a shattered leg, continued to fire a starboard pom-pom of which he had charge, and when the ship's electricity failed, went on firing with the hand-gear, till, wounded again in many places, he died by his gun. A battleship was sunk by a London stockbroker, and business men, it has been said, make good jungle-fighters.

For high technical efficiency coolly maintained in harassing or desperate circumstances, for dogged determination and a high degree of skill leading to success in operations, the Londoner seems to be outstanding and has received a remarkable number of awards. A few instances must serve to show what the modern Londoner, whose peace-time occupation may be of the most innocuous, has under his skin.

There was Flight-Sergeant Hazard of Harlesden (since killed, alas), who in an early raid on Milan with his craft under attack, in flames and

COLLECTING FIREWOOD IN BOMBED PIMLICO, 1942
Water Colour by Anthony Gross

with one engine failing, finding that one of his crew was wounded, decided not to abandon the craft and brought it back over the Alps to a safe landing. Flight-Sergeant Lipshitz, a salesman of Stepney "has never failed to fly his aircraft to the target and back though the craft has been severely damaged on several occasions." Pilot-Officer Hills, a cashier of Canning Town, Flight-Sergeants Cooper, gunner, a clerk of Chelsea, Edwards, a railway clerk of Limehouse, Cambridge, a fishmonger of Greenwich, were decorated for repeated successful attacks on the most heavily defended enemy targets. Flight-Sergeant Kempster, a packer of Ilford, wireless operator, when his pilot was killed outright saved the aircraft from crashing by instantly pulling back the control column ; and two Londoners were among those decorated for their work in the exceptional operation of bombing the Dams.

Excellent shooting was done by Aircraftsman Bullen of Islington who twice brought down dive-bombers by promptly manning his A.A. gun which was mounted on a lorry for evacuation in a great congestion of vehicles in the Libyan retreat, and by Sergeant Griffith a bank clerk of Muswell Hill who knocked out five tanks and damaged many more by holding his fire "in the coolest possible manner" till he was almost overrun.

Such instances can be repeated indefinitely, and each day adds to the long tale of resplendent deeds, in which outstanding talent as well as high heroism is shown. Fate has been kind to the Londoner, in bestowing upon him capacities equal to the great and grim occasions which have been not infrequent in his history, and to meet her sometimes exorbitant demands. And sometimes she wears an indulgent smile, as when the island of Lampedusa surrendered to Flight-Sergeant Cohen, a tailor's cutter of Clapton, landing somewhat unpremeditatedly in his Swordfish, and when Catania surrendered to young Mr. Gardner of Oddenino's.

To those who remember the last war and the soaked and bedraggled heroes of the Flanders mud, the contemporary hero seems a dandy. There are creases in battle-dress trousers, shoes are said to be shined and chins shaved in the intervals of operations, and there is a famous waxed moustache from Islington which in the whole of the Libyan campaigns, it is said, was never (literally or figuratively) let down. The fighting Londoner is a smart man and nine times out of ten he is mother's good boy.

During the earlier stages of the advance in Tunisia a correspondent noticed a little group of cockneys, who refused to move an inch under the day-long onslaught of German tanks and infantry. "Then tanks and panzer infantry came at us, and we got our guns on them, and fairly socked them," Captain Emerson, of London, said.

"And the men who had held the pass sat in the morning sunshine, writing letters home to say they were safe."

> "The angels keep their ancient places;
> Turn but a stone, and start a wing!
> 'Tis ye, 'tis your estranged faces,
> That miss the many-splendoured thing.
> But, (when so sad thou canst not sadder)
> Cry; and upon thy so sore loss
> Shall shine the traffic of Jacob's ladder
> Pitched between Heaven and Charing Cross."
>
> Francis Thompson.